The Mystery

Who Stole th
Prince Regent'

On 12th August 1812, th … n society were invited to the city of … the grandest social event of the decade; … Regent's 50th birthday party at the world fam… ssembly Rooms.

As a centrepiece for this lavish party, the Mayor of Bath planned to present a very special birthday gift to the Prince; a priceless golden statue that had recently been uncovered beneath the city's ancient streets. So secretive and valuable was this statue, that few people had seen it, some even believing that it didn't exist!

On the night of the party, as the city's Mayor removed the veil to present the gift, onlookers were stunned to see that the statue had been stolen, and replaced by a humble cabbage!

Who was responsible for this most daring and audacious heist?

Was it taken for financial gain? Did someone have a grudge against the Prince? Or did it simply not exist?

Solve the clues to eliminate suspects, identify the statue, and finally unravel this legendary Georgian mystery!

The story of the Prince's Stolen Statue detailed throughout this book is fictional, however the historical information and all extra details related to each clue is factual and based on detailed historical research.

HOW TO PLAY

1 Follow the Maps to find the location of your clue

2 Solve the Clue to eliminate one option from the list on page 1 (Extra help is on the back page)

3 At each stop you will Unravel more of the legendary tale.

4 At the end of your adventure your last remaining items on Page 1 will Reveal the final Secrets of the Mystery

IMPORTANT INFORMATION

1 On rare occasions, clues may be temporarily covered or permanently removed. In this instance we ask you to use the extra clues at the back of the book, and if possible, please report this to us.

It is recommended that you do the activity within 3 months of purchase, to reduce this risk.

2 Take care! You are responsible for yourself and your group. Be careful crossing roads, make sure to respect old monuments and private property, and if you are drinking alcohol please drink responsibly.

3 Any food & drink discounts available in this booklet are at the discretion of the stated premises, and may be subject to change or cancellation.

Directions to Starting Point

The starting point for the treasure hunt is the

[Crystal Palace pub](#),

10-11 Abbey Green, Bath BA1 1NW

Once arriving at the pub, you can begin your treasure hunt with your first clue!

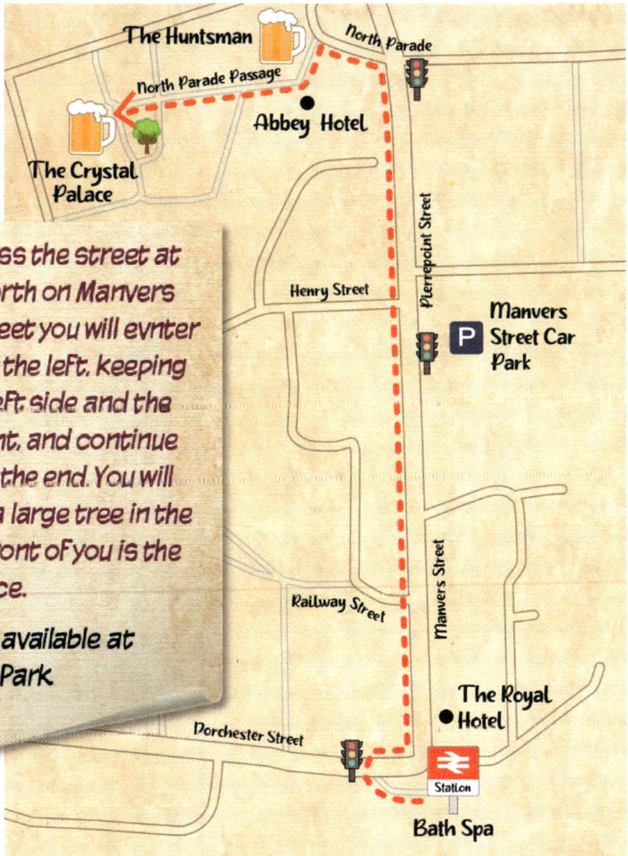

Exit Bath Spa station, cross the street at the traffic lights, head north on Manvers Street. At the top of the street you will evnter a large open area. Stick to the left, keeping the Abbey Hotel on your left side and the Huntsman pub on your right, and continue through the small alley to the end. You will emerge into a square with a large tree in the middle. The yellow pub in front of you is the Crystal Palace.

P Parking options are available at Manvers Street Car Park.

The Crystal Palace

Pub Stop 1

British Naval hero Horatio Nelson was a frequent visitor to Bath, often coming here to recuperate from exhausting campaigns away at sea. He was first sent here by his father in 1781, after a particularly difficult time serving in Nicaragua. On one particular visit to Bath, Nelson himself stayed at this very pub, which was known at the time as the 'Three Tuns Lodging' house.

Amazingly this site can be dated back nearly two thousand years, as a perfectly intact Roman mosaic floor was uncovered in the basement in the 1980's, which was not moved, but protected under a plastic sheet and layer of sand to remain preserved in the pub's cellar forever.

Clue 1

As you face the pub, on the right you will see Elton House.

Find the fire badge on the wall to decode the message and complete your first clue.

(Extra help on back page)

Eliminate a statue shape

Story

The night before his big birthday event, the prince arrived in Bath in his glittering royal carriage, but was met by a rather restless and agitated local crowd.

Some were upset by the large public expense that this party was costing them, while others couldn't bear the thought of a priceless local artefact being taken away to London by a 'selfish and greedy prince'.

Despite the frosty welcome, the prince and his entourage were determined to experience the best of Bath, and immediately hit the town for a night of drinking, dancing, and theatre.

Directions

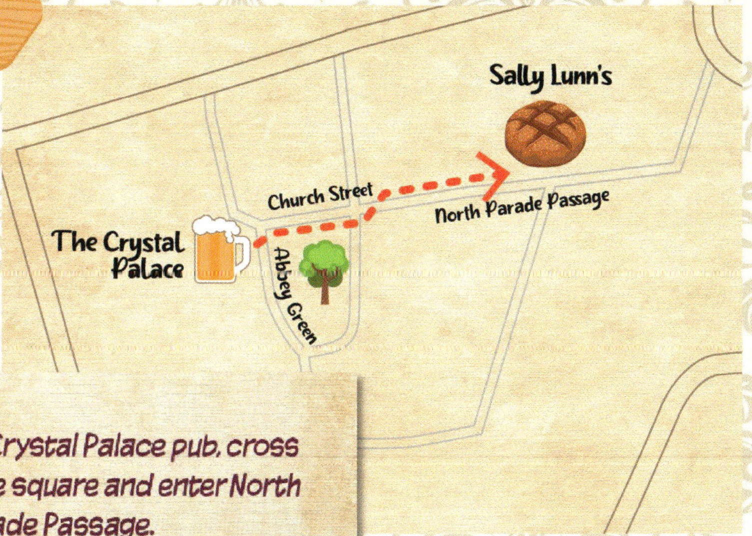

As you exit the Crystal Palace pub, cross the cobblestone square and enter North Parade Passage.

On your left you will see 'Sally Lunn's', which is the location of your next clue.

Sally Lunn's

Sally Lunn (or Solange Luyon) was a French Huguenot who fled her native land to avoid persecution; arriving in Bath in 1680. Shortly after her arrival, Sally Lunn started working in a bakery, and could often be seen selling bread from a basket around Bath Abbey. It was during this time that she introduced a French style brioche bun to the city, which quickly gained popularity as the Sally Lunn Bun.
The method of creating Lunn's trademark bun remained a hidden secret, however in 1937 while the house was being renovated, the original written recipe was discovered in a secret cupboard in the old wall panelling, which can now be found on display inside.

Clue 2

'Catching a thief can be quite a pane!'

First count the number of **individual panes of glass** in each area to find the values of: A ☐ B ☐ C ☐

Use these numbers in the equations below to **eliminate an invitation number:**

[A x B ☐ + C ÷ 2 ☐] x House number 4 = ☐

Story

On the morning of his party, the prince awoke with a rather sore head and requested 'one of those Sally Lunn buns' he had heard so much about in order to ease his pain.

Unfortunately the horses had not been prepped, so his young footman was ordered to 'fetch one in haste' at the prince's request.

After queuing in line like a commoner for over an hour, the sweaty and exhausted footman ran back to the royal residence to find the prince fast asleep on a full stomach!

Directions

Continue along North Parade Passage, and as you exit, follow the road round to the left until you enter York Street. Continue along York Street until you pass under an archway and into Stall Street. Turn right and you will see the King's and Queen's Baths on your right hand side.

Roman Baths

Long before the Romans arrived in Bath in AD44, this site was a valuable shrine of the ancient Celts, who worshipped the goddess Sulis here. The Romans therefore officially named the city 'Aquae Sulis' in honour of this Celtic deity, and combined her with their own goddess of wisdom, Minerva. Superstitious Romans at the time would write curses on sheets of lead and throw them in the spring, hoping that vengeance would be reaped upon those who had wronged them. Thousands of these have since been discovered, with many of them written in backwards writing so that only the goddess could read them. An amazingly preserved golden head of Sulis Minerva is on display in the museum.

Clue 3

Look at the outside of the King's and Queen's Baths. Inside the laurel at the top is the profile of a face looking at an animal.

Eliminate the animal from your list of statue shapes.

Story

After emerging from his slumber, the prince was invited to embark on a busy schedule of local sight-seeing, starting with the famous Roman Baths.

Whilst bathing in the healing pools was considered the perfect cure for the 'overindulgence of alcohol', the prince refused to try it for himself, through fear of appearing in another harmful satirical cartoon; the kind of which that tormented him throughout his lifetime.

He did however agree to taste the water, remarking that 'it wasn't to his liking', much to the displeasure of the city's Mayor who saw it as a PR disaster.

Directions

Continue along Stall Street and turn right between the columns and head towards the Abbey. Follow the Abbey around to the left. Keep the Abbey on your right and head towards the green trees in the distance. Keep the gardens on your right, and follow the road until you reach Pulteney Bridge. Your next clue is halfway along the bridge.

Pulteney Bridge

When wealthy and privileged young men 'came of age' in the 18th century (typically 21), many embarked on a 'Grand Tour' of Europe. Such trips inspired the splendid architecture we associate with the Georgian period, and Pulteney Bridge is a classic example. Built in 1769 in the Palladian style, this 41 metre bridge was funded by the man reported to be the wealthiest in Britain at the time, William Pulteney, who spent £10,000 on the project (several million pounds in today's money). It is one of only four bridges in the world to have shops lining both sides; the other three are the Ponte Vecchio in Florence, the Rialto in Venice, and Erfurt's Kramerbrucke in Erfurt, Germany.

Clue 4

Find this plaque which is displayed close to the centre of Pulteney Bridge.

The letters marked by a red X will spell out details of your next **hiding place to eliminate.**

ELIMINATE

Be careful of the road!

THIS BRIDGE WAS BUILT IN 1774
TO THE DESIGN OF

ROBERT ADAM

IT WAS MUCH ALTERED IN THE
19TH CENTURY AND THE SOUTH
WEST END WAS SHORTENED IN 1908

THE DOWNSTREAM ELEVATION
WAS RESTORED IN 1951 AND THE
PIERS WERE XXXXXPINNED IN 1971

IN 1975 EUROPEAN ARCHITECTURAL
HERITAGE YEAR, XXX SHOP FACADES
WERE REPAIRED AND PXXXLY REXXXXXD
BY THE

GEORGIAN GROUP

IN ASSOCIATION WITH THE
COLBY TRUST & BATH CITY COUNCIL
WITH A SUBSTANTIAL GRANT FROM
HER MAJESTY 'S GOVERNMENT

Story

Following his tour of the Baths, the prince climbed aboard his royal barge and headed to see Pulteney Bridge in all its splendour.

However as he disembarked, a strong and unexpected wind blew the prince off balance, and it was only the quick thinking actions of his footman who managed to catch him before he fell into the river below.

Rather than thanking him, the prince scolded the footman for tearing his waistcoat and teased him for his small stature.

Directions

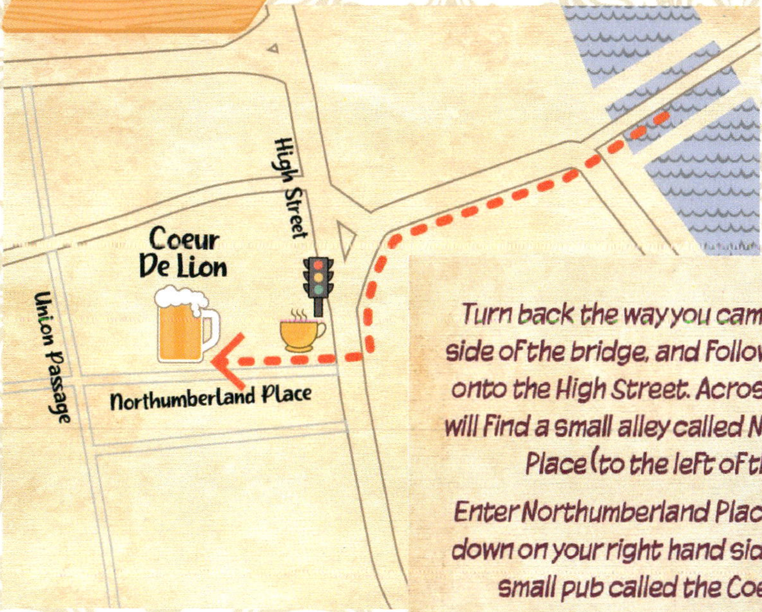

Turn back the way you came to the same side of the bridge, and follow the main road onto the High Street. Across the road you will find a small alley called Northumberland Place (to the left of the Café).

Enter Northumberland Place, and halfway down on your right hand side you will see a small pub called the Coeur De Lion.

Coeur de Lion

Pub Stop 2

'Coeur de Lion' meaning 'lionheart' in French, holds the title of being the city's smallest pub, and is reported to be the only drinking establishment in the country to bear this unusual name. When Richard I, also known as Richard the Lionheart, was returning from fighting in the crusades he was captured in a well staged ambush, and held for ransom by the German Emperor. In the famous stories of Robin Hood, Richard made it back to the country safely, to overthrow his tyrannical brother King John. This heroic image of Richard I may have been an early example of PR management by his mother Eleanor, in order to soften the blow of the huge ransom paid by the people of the Plantagenet lands to free him from capture.

Clue 5

Your next clue can be found on this page, hidden between a well and a bush.

(You don't need to find anything at the location to solve this clue)

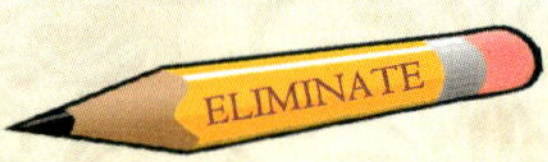

Eliminate a statue shape

Story

On the night before the prince's birthday party, the city's pubs were packed and buzzing with the sound of gossip, rumour and discontent.

In one particular pub it was reported by the landlady that she overheard a voice exclaiming 'the prince won't get his hands on our precious statue, he will be leaving this city empty handed! I can promise you that!'.

While no physical description was given, the landlady confirmed that it was spoken in a local Somerset accent.

Directions

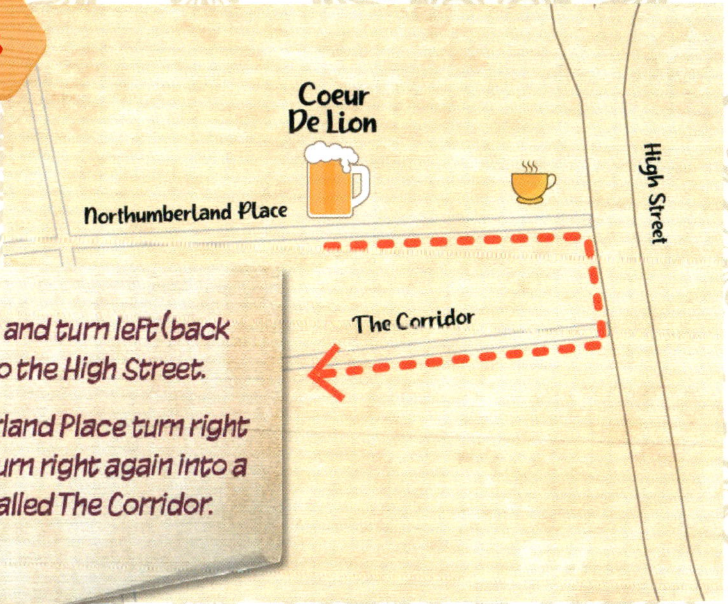

Exit the Coeur de Lion and turn left (back the way you came) to the High Street.

As you exit Northumberland Place turn right and then immediately turn right again into a small passageway called The Corridor.

The Corridor

Built in 1825, 'The Corridor' is one of the world's earliest retail arcades, following the hugely popular Galeries des Bois in Paris, and London's fashionable Burlington Arcade. When originally opened, an orchestra would have regularly entertained customers from the balcony above, and the shops would have been guarded by a 'Corridor Constable', who could have been easily spotted on patrol with his maroon suit, black top hat and cane. Tragically the first ever 'Corridor Constable' died on duty, after falling through a shop trap door while helping a trader with a delivery.

Clue 6

To solve the mystery,
you'll find clues,
in a range of different places.
Look up high,
and you will see,
a thousand animal faces.

Eliminate a hiding place

Story

As his birthday party drew nearer, the prince had a small window in his schedule for some late afternoon shopping, where he could browse local trinkets and the latest fashionable items in the city's most desirable boutiques.

It was while out shopping that he had a chance encounter with a childhood friend, a famous dandy and fashionista who he had studied with as a young boy.

The prince eagerly invited him to his evening party, unaware that the dandy held a longstanding grudge against him for mocking his dress sense in front of their mutual acquaintances. He had always vowed to get his revenge!

Directions

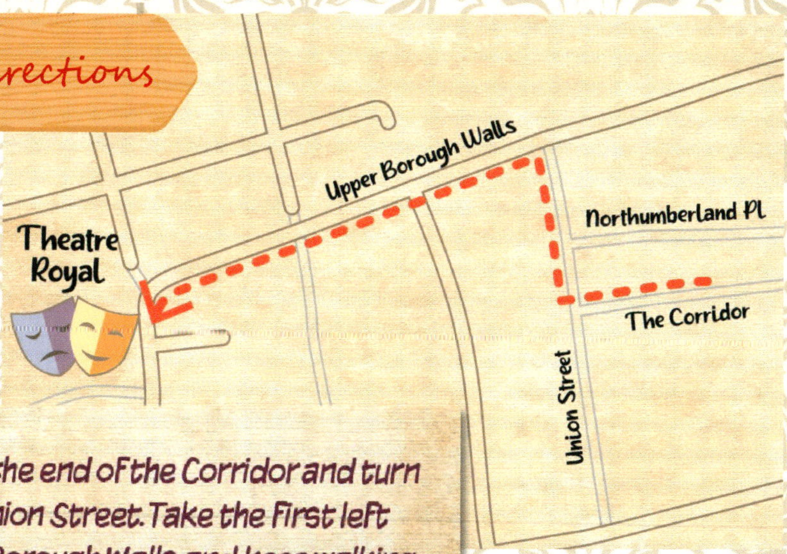

Continue to the end of the Corridor and turn right on Union Street. Take the first left onto Upper Borough Walls and keep walking to the end where you will see a large open area. Your next clue is at the Theatre Royal, which lies just after the bend in the road.

Theatre Royal

Built in 1805, Bath's Theatre Royal has been described as one of the most important surviving examples of Georgian theatre in the country. The building is allegedly haunted by an old 'grey lady', the ghost of a theatre regular who would often watch performances from her favourite top box seat. Legend has it that she fell for a local young actor, however when her love went unrequited she hung herself from the back of the door in her room in the Garrick's Head pub across the road. People who have seen her describe feeling an immediate sense of depression, as if they have absorbed her sadness.

Clue 7

All of these are Shakespeare plays:

1.  4th letter ☐

2.  10th letter ☐

3.  1st letter ☐

4.  4th letter ☐

5.  6th letter ☐

6.  3rd letter ☐

Take the letters detailed above (**don't include 'the'**) to make a six-letter word, and eliminate the suspect most closely associated with it.

Eliminate a suspect

Story

On his drunken night out the day before his party, the prince had attended Bath's Theatre Royal to watch a performance of Richard III in front of a sell-out crowd. While he was not particularly interested in high culture, the actress playing Queen Elizabeth caught his eye, and she was invited to the Royal Box to meet the prince himself. He loved showing off and mixing with common actresses, and quickly asked her to be his date for his big birthday party. Little did he know however that this particular actress had a reputation for drunkenness and theft, and had spent much of her youth in jail!

Directions

Head back the way you came along Upper Borough Walls, and stop at the entrance of Trim Bridge on your left hand side (black bollards in front).

Your next clue is above the door of the building on the left hand side of the entrance to Trim Bridge.

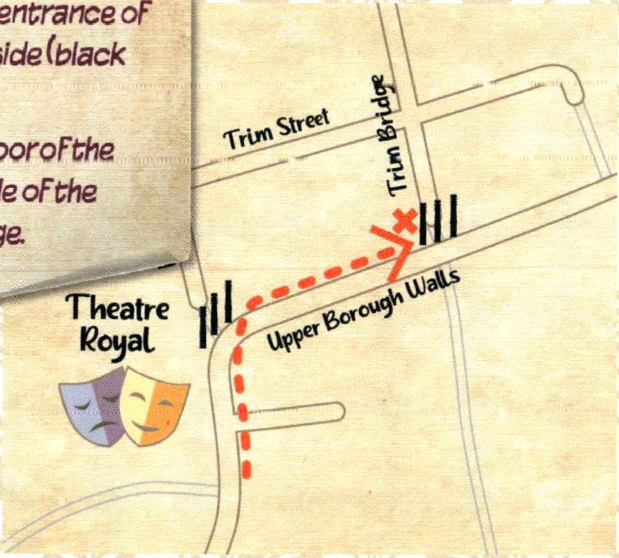

Jane Austen

Jane Austen moved to Bath in 1801 after her father decided to retire in the city and move the family away from their rural home in Hampshire. She resided in a number of the city's residences, including number 25 Gay Street in 1805. She had a colourful social life, regularly attending balls at the Assembly Rooms & Pump Rooms, and set two of her novels here ('Northanger Abbey' and 'Persuasion'). When first arriving in Bath she said she would do 'everything in her power' to avoid living in the rough and deprived area of 'Trim Street', however after her father's death led to financial difficulties this was her last known address before she left the city to live in Clifton, Bristol.

Clue 8

Use the 10 gold recessed letters above the door of the cream building to the left of the black bollards to eliminate an invitation number.

S P M

___ ___ ___

ELIMINATE

Eliminate an invitation number

Story

To ensure a positive image of Bath and to keep the prince happy, an attempt was made to limit the amount of newspaper reporters in the city, and to control the content of the stories that were printed. Unfortunately prior to the prince's arrival a satirical cartoon had been circulated, depicting him as highwayman, holding up the city of Bath with a pistol and escaping with the golden statue.

This cartoon was one of the factors later identified as a cause for local unrest on the streets and for the prince's widespread unpopularity in the lead up to his party.

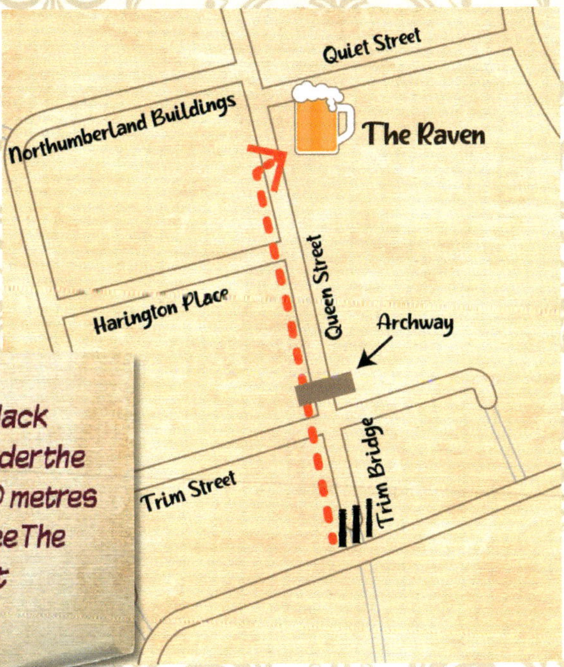

Directions

Enter Trim Bridge through the black bollards, and continue straight under the archway into Queen Street. After 20 metres on your right hand side you will see The Raven pub, which is your next stopping point.

The Raven

Prior to being known as 'The Raven', this pub was called 'Hatchett's Wine Lodge'. Legend has it that a former landlord of the pub murdered his wife with a hatchet, and hence the pub became known by this grisly nickname.
Another less gruesome theory is that it was named after London's 'Hatchett's Hotel' from which the characters in Charles Dickens' novel Pickwick Papers left from on their journey to Bath.

Clue 9

People flocked from all over the country to join the prince's party. Use the pictures above to decipher the British place names. **Eliminate a hiding place** associated with the 5-letter word spelt vertically in blue boxes.

ELIMINATE

Story

If the party was such a controversial and potentially dangerous event then why hold it at all?

Many spa towns of the Georgian period notoriously experienced a boom-and-bust existence, and those financially invested in Bath were fearful that the city might go the same way. Property speculators had run up huge debts, and they were desperate to guarantee long-term prosperity. The Mayor of Bath was one of those heavily invested and was rumoured to be close to bankruptcy. It was hoped that royal support from the prince, along with large swathes of wealthy visitors would guarantee the city's fortunes.

Directions

Exit the Raven pub and turn right and then left into Wood Street / Northumberland Buildings. At the end of the short street you will see a large park called Queen Square.

Head towards a large stone obelisk in the centre of the square which is the location of your next clue.

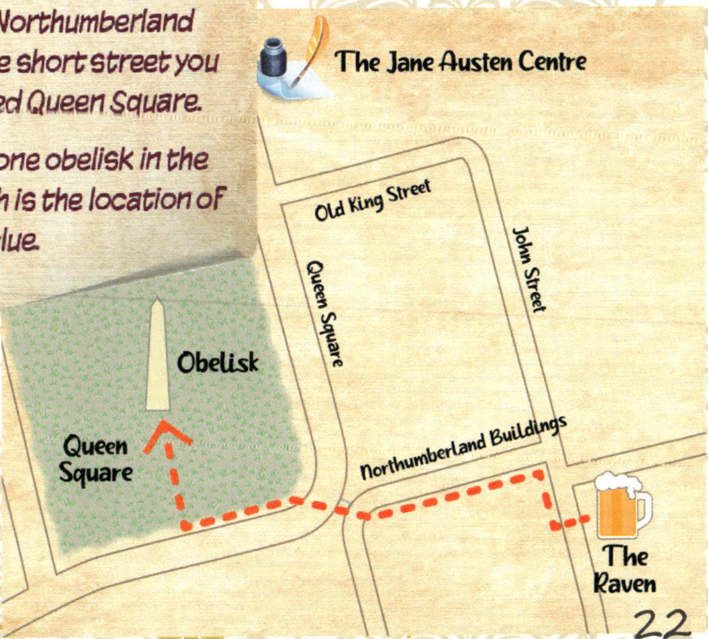

Queen Square

Queen Square was the work of famous Bath resident and architect John Woods (designer of The Royal Crescent), who himself lived at number 9.
Whilst being a master architect, we was notoriously outspoken, impatient, and difficult to deal with. In one particular uninspiring council meeting he stood up and shouted 'All I want is names for my three streets!'. Legend has it that someone yelled 'Quiet John Woods!', which inspired him to name the square's adjoining roads 'Quiet Street, John Street and Wood Street'.

Clue 10

Find the year (in Roman numerals) that the central obelisk was erected by Richard Nash, to calculate the total and eliminate an invitation number.

V = 3

X = 5

D = 70

I = 2

M = 150

C = 20

___ ___ ___

Eliminate an invitation number

ELIMINATE

Story

The 'party of the decade' attracted a socially elite crowd who travelled to Bath from all corners of the country. Many of the large private houses in Queen's Square were rented out to visiting dignitaries who jostled for space in this prestigious neighbourhood.

It was no accident that most guests were drafted in from far away places. The majority of local Bath residents were strongly against the decision to gift the statue to the prince, with some royal guards fearing riots or attempts to sabotage the prince's special event.

Directions

Exit the square into the main road (Queen Square) and head north across the traffic lights into Gay Street. At the end of the road you will emerge into one of Bath's most famous landmarks: The Circus.

Your next clue can be found among the houses numbered 1 to 9, which are on your left hand side as you enter The Circus.

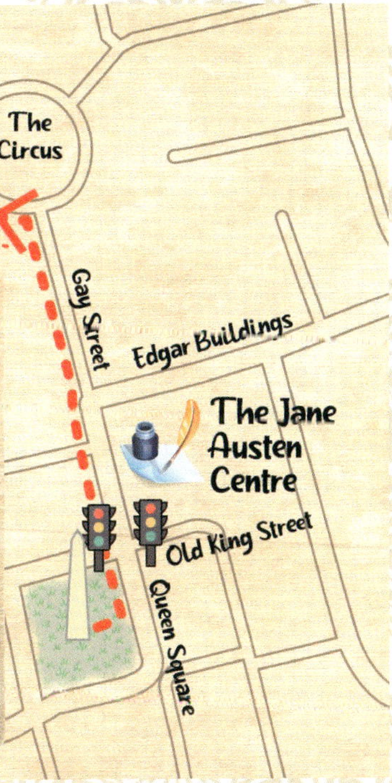

The Circus

It is said that the architect of this amazing site John Wood was fascinated by the Druids, evidence of which can be found in many parts of the design of this Circus.
The central grassy area shares the exact same diameter as Stonehenge (318ft) which is a key Druid shrine. It has also been said that his designs were based on Druid worship of the skies, with the Circus representing the sun, and his other project, the Royal Crescent, representing the moon. You will also see lots of Druid symbolism in the carvings above the doors of the houses, including trees, acorns, and serpents.

Clue 11

You will find a range of stone symbols running along the side of the houses. Match the symbols to a house number to create a 3-digit number.

Only look at houses numbered 1-9, and only consider the 4 symbols directly above each door.

___ ___ ___

Eliminate an invitation number

Story

It was while excavating this area for the building of the circus, that a number of valuable Celtic relics were discovered in the earth; one of which was rumoured to be a priceless solid gold statue in the form of an animal. To prevent it from being stolen, precise details of the statue were kept secret, including its physical appearance and location. However it was not only its monetary value that made it so special. The Druids (the learned class among the ancient Celts) believed that the statue possessed a strong mystical power, and therefore the Chief of the Druids was invited to the party to present the statue to the prince.

Directions

Follow the bend around the Circus and enter Brock Street. Keep walking to the end of the street and you will emerge in front of Bath's most famous and iconic landmark, 'The Royal Crescent'. Your next clue can be found at Number 1.

Royal Crescent

The Royal Crescent was completed in 1774 and is formed of 30 Grade I listed properties. Given the strict controls over the alteration of Grade I buildings, a huge controversy was caused in 1972 when resident Amabel Edmunda Wellesley Colley decided to paint her front door a shade of primrose yellow. She defended her action, stating that as a descendent of the Duke of Wellington (her great grandfather) she was entitled to paint it in his favourite colour. The issue was so contentious that it was raised in the House of Commons, with the decision going in Ms Colley's favour. Since then, the door at number 22 has remained in this colour as a tradition, and in honour of Ms Colley's victory.

Clue 12

Find the plaque on the outside of the former house of George Saintsbury.

Take the 16 letters below his name, and place them in order in the sentence below to eliminate a suspect.

_OR_ID _ __YOR WITH

DIS___OUR, LEGA__Y HE _I_

____LE RIGHT.

Eliminate a suspect

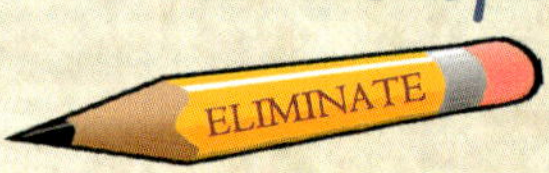

Story

Around two months prior to the big event, a plan was hatched in one of the exclusive residences in the Royal Crescent between the Mayor of Bath and one of the Prince Regent's royal representatives for a deal to be made; The prince would be treated to a lavish birthday party at public expense and be gifted the priceless golden statue, and in return he would award the city the name 'Royal Bath' and the Mayor would receive a knighthood. The deal would have been seen by many as a terrible sell-out, however the Mayor kept the details under lock and key, only to be released after the big event.

✓ **Take a photo**

✓ **Tag on social media: @mysteryguides**

For a chance to win a prize!!

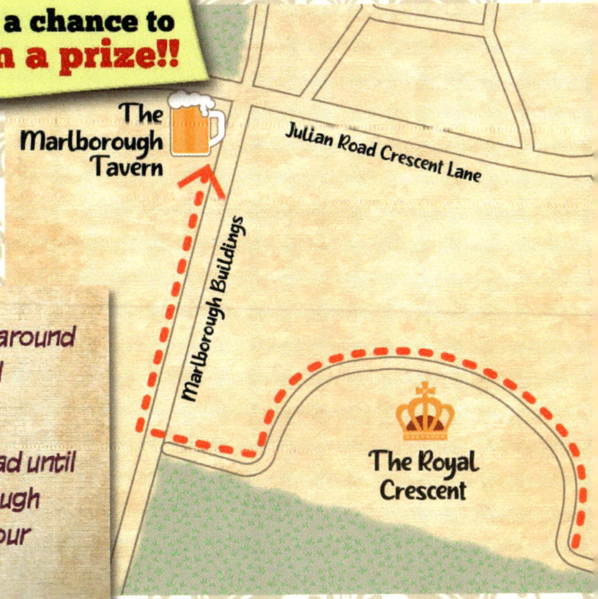

Directions

Follow the Royal Crescent all the way around and you will enter a road called Marlborough Buildings.

Turn right, and continue along the road until you see a pub called The Marlborough Tavern, which is the location of your next clue.

Marlborough Tavern

Pub Stop 4

In the 18th century, the wealthy residents of the Royal Crescent and surrounding neighbourhoods would pay 'soil men' to dispose of the contents of their potties, who did so before 5am so that the smell would have dispersed by the time they awoke. The problem is that the soil men dumped this waste just to the west of the Crescent and the smell often blew into the heart of the neighbourhood. To counter this problem, the Marlborough Buildings (where you are now) were built in an attempt to create a barrier. Locals say that the present vegetable allotments that sit on the old dumping ground are the most fertile in the city.

Clue 13

Find 6 vegetables hidden in this grid.

Take the last letter of each word, to make a 6-letter word.

_ _ _ _ _ _ _ _ _

_ _ _ _ _ _ _ _ _

_ _ _ _ _ _ _ _ _

_ _ _ _ _ _ _ _ _ _ _ _

_ _ _ _ _ _

_ _ _ _ _ _

A	J	G	I	N	G	E	R	C	F	R
K	B	I	H	L	O	Q	A	D	E	G
B	R	J	E	M	P	R	B	W	H	I
Y	O	K	G	T	D	S	O	E	M	J
Z	C	L	F	N	O	L	Z	L	U	K
T	C	I	F	M	F	M	Y	M	S	N
U	O	S	G	I	A	B	A	O	H	P
V	L	R	L	C	C	T	X	T	R	R
W	I	U	H	N	Q	U	W	Q	O	S
X	A	D	E	O	P	V	Q	T	O	V
C	U	C	U	M	B	E	R	U	M	W

Eliminate a suspect holding this item

ELIMINATE

Story

Very few people had ever laid eyes on the mysterious statue, and prior to the party it was encased in a solid metal box and kept under 24-hour armed guard.

The thief therefore must have had close and private access to the statue prior to it being revealed.

There was only really one person who had the motive and opportunity to snatch the statue, and that is one of the two remaining suspects on your list. A number of other questions however also remain; how did they do it? What was their motive? And what did the statue look like?

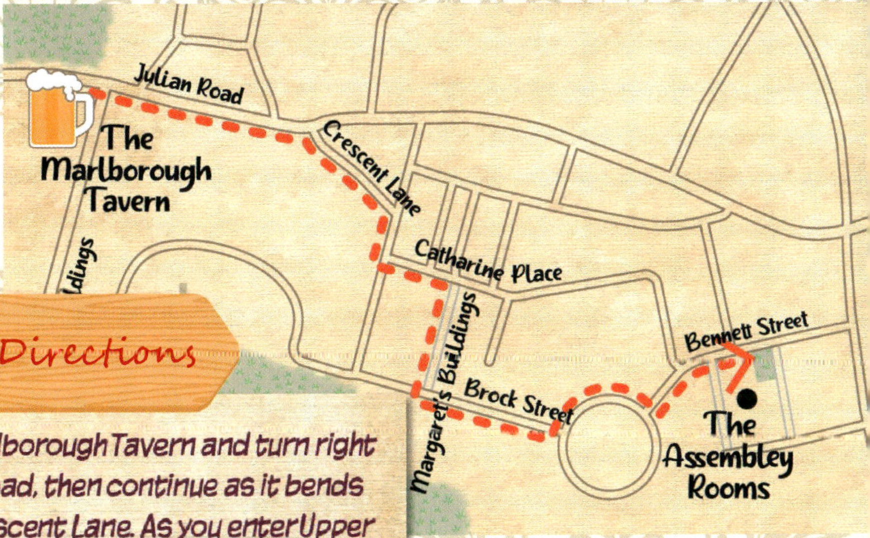

Directions

Leave the Marlborough Tavern and turn right into Julian Road, then continue as it bends right into Crescent Lane. As you enter Upper Church Street take a quick left into Catherine Place and then right through the black bollards into a small street called Margaret's Buildings. Head back to the Circus via Brock Street and Follow it round into Bennett Street. Across the road you will see Bath's Assembley Rooms. Your next clue is located in a small garden at the rear.

Assembly Rooms

In its day, the Assembly Rooms was the centre of fashionable Georgian society, hosting between 800-1,200 guests in its four rooms; the Ballroom the Tea Room, The Octagon, and the Card Room.

Its official purpose was to provide 'the general meeting of polite persons of both sexes, for the sake of conversation, gallantry, news and play', and was therefore a great place to meet a partner (mothers were known to bring their daughters here in order to meet eligible young men). You will see that the windows are deliberately set up high in order to protect its patrons from the peering eyes of nosey commoners hoping to catch a glimpse into these exclusive high society events.

Clue 14

In the garden of the Assembly Rooms is a strange round sculpture. Find who it is dedicated to, to complete the clue below.

The ? *Memorial Sculpture*

Crack the code:

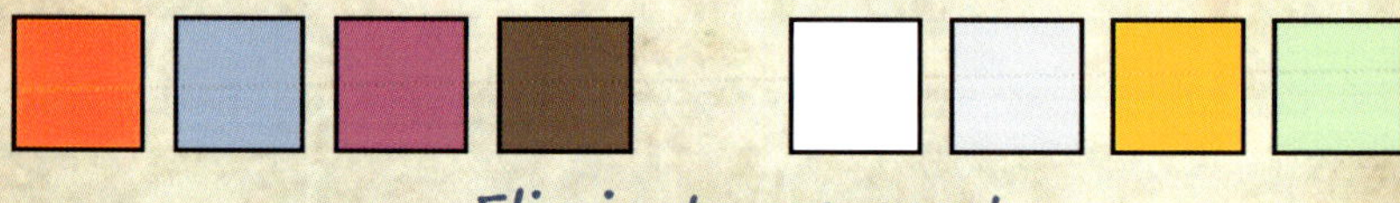

Eliminate a suspect

Story

The Mayor of Bath was so determined to make the big birthday event as smooth as possible that he insisted all the decoration and furniture for the party was in place three hours before the prince arrived; that included having the statue in place on its plinth, covered by a velvet veil. This was the opportunity that the thief was waiting for. Requesting a final moment of private prayer to the mystical statue, the Druid quickly switched the statue for a cabbage that he had concealed beneath his robes, and swiftly headed for the exit. He would return to the venue sometime later after hiding the statue, to avoid any suspicion.

Directions

Next to the memorial garden is a small alley called Saville Row. Head south along this alley into Bartlett Street, and continue down the hill until you reach George Street. Take a quick right, cross the traffic lights, and then turn left into Milsom Street, which is the location of your next clue.

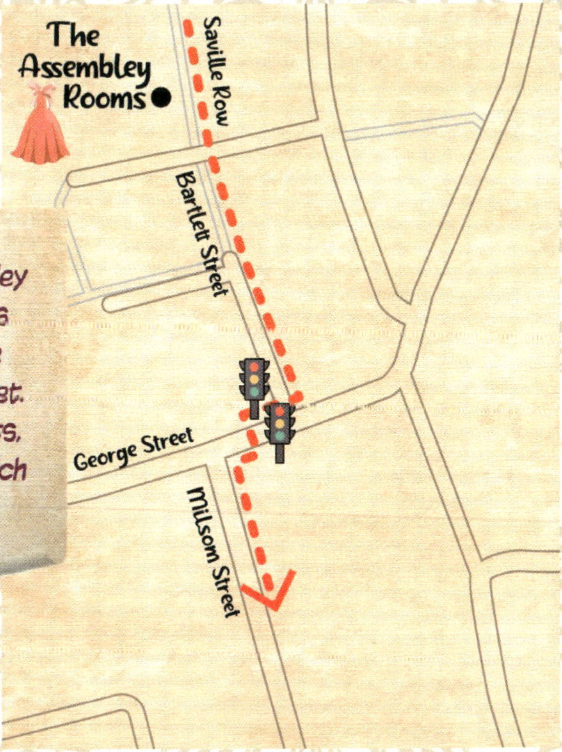

Milsom Street

The grand buildings you see lining either side of Milsom Street were originally built as large and luxurious townhouses, however sometime after, the area was transformed into a high-end shopping street. Such was its notoriety for luxury, the street featured Jane Austen's 'Northanger Abbey' as one of the most opulent areas in the city.

Clue 15

Your next clue can be found somewhere in this stretch of Milsom Street.

As you walk south, look to your left, for columns in brown and red stone. Facing the front, look high and right, for faded lettering that is still shown.

Eliminate a hiding place

Story

Upon discovering that the statue had been stolen the Mayor enforced a city-wide lockdown in order to prevent it from being smuggled out of Bath. An army of investigators trawled the streets looking for information on its whereabouts, and a huge cash reward was offered for its safe return. However, given that most locals wanted to keep the statue out of the hands of the prince, nobody was forthcoming. The only reported sighting of the thief was given by a young chimneysweep who said that he saw a strange old man running down Milsom Street carrying something beneath his clothes, but was unable to formally identify him.

Continue along Milsom Street and take the First left into Green Street. You will se a small pub on your right hand side called 'The Old Green Tree' which is your final destination, and hiding place of the golden statue.

Directions

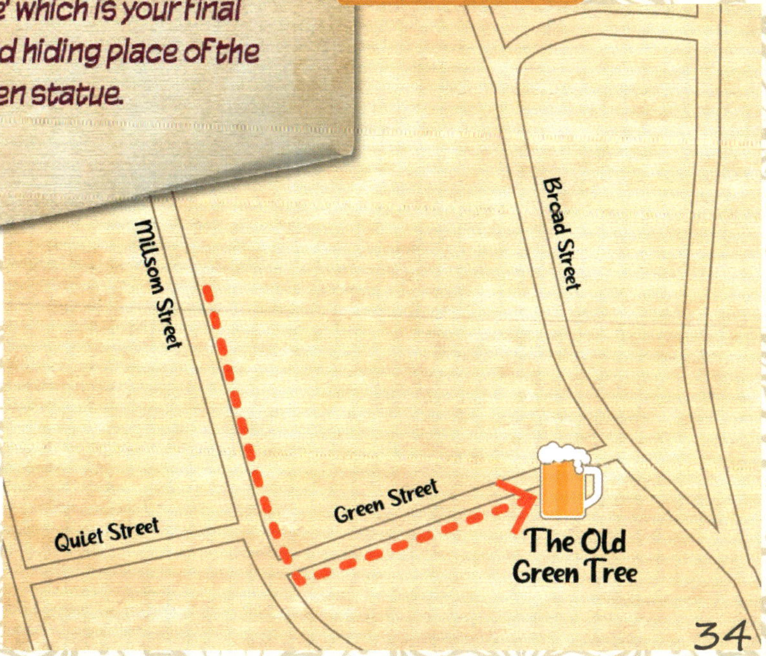

The Old Green Tree

Pub Stop 5

This pub dates back to 1716, when a milliner called John Cornish bought part of the land to start building Green Street.
The pub takes its name from a large and beloved oak tree which towered over an old bowling green which sat on this very spot. The Old Green Tree once operated its own brewery on the premises, which produced its own beer until the early 20th century.

Clue 16

Your final statue shape to eliminate can be found somewhere on the cover of this book!

Eliminate a statue shape

Story

In order to protect the statue and ensure that it wasn't recovered by the authorities, the decision was made by the Council of the Druids to bury the statue beneath their headquarters, The Old Green Tree. Its location became a sworn secret of the organisation, which was not revealed until after the death of their Chief several decades later. The last question that remains in this mystery is why was the statue stolen by the Druids? Why was their leader willing to risk his life to save this peculiar golden statue?

Turn over the page for the final chapter of this epic Georgian mystery!

You have solved all of the clues and completed the mystery! However one question remains:

Why was the statue stolen?

The final chapter..

The image of a cockerel had an extremely sacred meaning to the ancient Druids, who believed that its morning crow had the power to ward off evil spirits. It was thought that if the golden cockerel was taken away from its original resting place, then bad luck and misery would forever plague the city of Bath.

The theft of the statue therefore was not seen as a crime against the prince, but more of a heroic act to save the future safety and prosperity of local residents.

After his death in 1840, the Chief Druid was exposed as the thief and hailed as a local hero for saving the fate of the city. It was decreed that the statue should forever remain in The Old Green Tree, and has been kept here ever since. The City Mayor however did not leave such an admirable legacy. Shortly after the prince's party he was exposed for corruption and stealing public finances and sentenced to ten years in jail.

Since the theft of the prince's statue, the cockerel has always held a special meaning for the residents of Bath, who upon hearing its crow feel a sense of comfort and traditionally raise a glass to their Druid hero.